The Ultimate Guide to Disney Photography

About the Book

Knowing how to take photos in certain areas is a necessity for any photographer, amateur and professional alike. Some locations around the world require just basic knowledge of photography techniques. Places like Disney World though, are unique in this aspect, as they are extremely diverse, featuring uniquely varying conditions in lighting and coloration.

Now, while you may have a digital camera in your pocket or around your neck and you may be aware of the fundamental rules of photography and how to apply them, you will need more than those if you truly wish to capture the essence of Disney.

This book is intended to teach you to do just that, revealing to you the photographic possibilities that you can take advantage of on your next visit.

Whether you are a professional photographer working on a project, or an amateur enthusiast simply looking to make the most of your trip to Disney World, this book can help you learn how to bring some of the magic of the venue into your images.

Some of the things that you will learn through this book include how to photograph certain events and shows, what settings to use in which areas, rides and lighting conditions, as well as some of the best locations for photos.

Keep in mind that the settings described in the book are based around digital SLR cameras. Non-SLR cameras may not feature some of the options mentioned here. For optimal advantage, it is advised to have a DSLR camera with you on your visits to Disney World.

Contents

Introduction

Disney World is known by many children as well as grown-ups, as the land of wonder, fantasy and adventure, a place of fairy-tale beauty and childlike charm like no other. And while at that most magical of places, it is considered almost a sin to not take any photos.

The memories that you can take back with you from what is considered the happiest, most magical place on planet earth, hold tremendous value to the heart. The very nature of the place dictates that you preserve happy memories in the form of visual presentations.

It is relatively easy to take good pictures while at Disney. The locations, the colors and the lighting, all are automatically ideal for photos.

The way the structures are arranged, the manner in which the characters carry themselves and all the bright colors that you can see on every street corner are all extremely suitable for photography. However, even though the entire magical kingdom makes for magical pictures no matter what camera equipment you are using or what skill level you possess, you simply have to improve your photography techniques, to take full advantage of the beauty.

Following are some additional reasons why improving and developing your photography skills for the sole purpose of taking better pictures can be of advantage to you as a photographer.

- The theme of the venue itself is based upon animated movies. Movies themselves are based upon the principles of composition and framing. Therefore, the venue is shaped ideally for better composition of photos. This allows you to further improve your composing skills.
- The characters are required to behave and carry themselves in a certain way. Also, they are required to pose as their animated counterparts. This makes them perfect subjects for photography as they are not only well versed in appearing in front of cameras, but they can provide for some great fashion photography practice.
- Disney features some brilliant low-light photography locations and opportunities. Many of the locations within the parks are beautifully lit with vibrantly colored lights. This will let you improve your low-light photography, making you a well rounded photographer.
- Group shots of family and friends are a must while at Disney. Even some characters walk around in groups and immediately pose for photos when asked. This makes it a perfect opportunity to improve your group shots. These techniques will aid you in other forms of group photography such as weddings and event photography as well.
- Many of the rides and attractions are moving at a pace. This requires expertise in moving shots and action photography during rides, to prevent blurry images, especially at night. Learning how to deal with such conditions will help you take much better action shots in the future.

Now that you know the advantages of learning how to take better photos at Disney World, as well as the infinite beauty that you can capture, let us move on to how you can do all of that and more.

Ideal Equipment for Disney Photography

Determining the ideal camera for the occasion is the very first step that you need to take. This is also the most subjective of steps, as you will have to decide what level of expertise and photographic excellence you need to achieve.

To this end, there are a variety of options at your disposal. From point-and-shoot cameras to higher end equipment such as DSLRs, to even mirrorless cameras; the list goes on. To aid you in your decision, you can look at what kind of photography will you be pursuing while at the venue.

Will you be taking simple family photos and a few close-ups?Will you be snapping away at everything you see?Or will you making a high quality, high resolution album of your adventures? Answering these questions can aid you in the decision.

If you will be doing the first, any camera, even the one in your smartphone, will be sufficient. For slightly better quality images, you can go for a compact digital camera, which will have a range of different options for you to play with as well. But if you want to take the best quality images possible, as is the intention behind this book, you will need a digital single lens reflex (DSLR) camera, complete with several lenses and accessories.

Lenses are arguably the most important aspect of the DSLR. Especially in the variety of situations and photo opportunities that are present at Disney, lenses will play a very significant part in bringing out the true beauty behind every scene.

Accessories such as a tripod, several image filters, a good flash and a strong, durable camera bag are necessary for more convenience and photographic variety.

Cameras

This is a purely subjective decision, depending on your desired photo quality, resolution, and scale. As mentioned, this guide is centered towards the more nuanced and detailed capturing potential of the DSLR. Keeping that in mind, following are the 10 best camera choices for you, when visiting Disney.

Entry Level

- **Canon EOS Rebel SL1/ EOS 100D:** The very basic but by no means an underperforming camera, this piece is perfect for those enthusiastic about photography yet leaning towards the more affordable side. The 18 megapixel sensor and the 1080p video make this a competent package for the price, not to mention the compact size and ergonomics.
- **Nikon D3400:** A slightly more advanced entry, the D3400 packs a potent punch with its 24.2 megapixel sensor and the superb autofocus. While this is more expensive than some of the other entry level DSLRs, it is nevertheless a wonderful piece of kit.
- **Canon EOS Rebel T6s/ EOS 760D:** With a price point bordering on the mid-range DSLR, the 760D might not be the first choice for a complete beginner or early enthusiast. However, the Flawless sensor, commendable handling and the additional LCD display make this not only more convenient, but more feature packed than the other entries on the list.

Mid-Range

- **Nikon D7200:** The surprisingly affordable and brilliantly featured D7200 is the ideal camera for anyone looking to take professional quality images with imaging equipment that costs less than half the price. Vibrant colors and a long battery life are just some of the features that make this system worth the cost of investing a little more.
- **Sony Alpha a77 Mark II:** If a lightning fast and precise autofocus and equally fast continuous shooting speeds are what you are looking for, look no further that the a77 Mark II. This camera is perhaps the best choice of equipment for fast paced photos such as those on rides or while moving. The 24.3 megapixel sensor rounds off the package par excellence.
- **Canon EOS 7D Mark II:** A bit more expensive than what you would expect of a mid-range DSLR, it is a brilliant camera nonetheless. What makes this system superior is the versatility that it brings, with portraits, landscapes and low-light images all in its expertise. The level of detail you can get on surfaces such as painted wood and cobbled ground is astounding, plus the vividness of the colors is beyond comparison in this range.

High End

- **Canon EOS 5DS:** The 50 megapixel sensor on the 5DS is reason enough why you should go for this camera if you are looking for something on the high end. By far the best for wide, sweeping shots and beautiful landscapes, this is one system that can truly capture the vibrancy of the venue. The price of the camera, while high, offers the best value for money, all things considered.
- **Nikon D810:** If you want your camera to be tough as well as packed with resolution as well as a killer autofocus system, the D810 is the kit for you. Built to last while containing all the elements that make for a great camera, the D810 is ideal for high-fidelity images including stunning portraits and incredibly detailed landscapes.
- **Canon EOS 5D Mark IV:** This is as complete a package as you could hope for in a camera. Also, this is the only camera up till now that can shoot video in 4K. Be it daytime portraits, or the nighttime fireworks show, you can be sure that you won't lose a single detail with this system. The price is considerably high and the performance is suited only for experts and those wanting to take professional quality photos.
- **Nikon D5:** If low light photography is your thing, then the D5 will excel over all others. The ISO range makes sure that even when there are minimal light conditions, the photos come out bright as well as reasonably detailed. This makes the D5 great for colorfully lit imagery in the night.

Lenses

Lenses are what make the DSLRso versatile and significant to the art of photography. There are a variety of lenses available for different purposes and different genres of photography. For Disney photography in particular, following is the ideal lens set that you should have, to make the most of your trip and get some wonderful pictures.

50mm f/1.4: This lens is the best possible tool for portraits due to its extremely shallow depth of field and the ability to place the entirety of the focus on the subject, with minimal distractions. If you plan to take lots of close-ups of the characters with a professional photographer's portraiture style, be sure to add this lens to your kit.

18-200mm f/3.5: The zoom range on this lens gives you the opportunity to capture those faraway spots or scenery that you cannot get up close to. Additionally, the lower end of the range gives you a wider angle, letting you capture more of the scene in front of you.

28-75mm f/2.8: While this lens makes for a mid-way point between the range of the earlier lens, it is the 2.8 aperture available at 75mm, which is the reason why you can get some amazingly composed shots in low light, from this lens. If you have a high-end, full frame camera, this is one of the more cost-effective options, lens wise.

14mm f/2.8: A combination of a wide angle and a wide aperture, this lens will let you capture wider shots in low light. A lot of the structures within Disney are brightly illuminated at night, making this a very valuable piece to have in a kit, if you intend to take landscapes as well as bright group shots at night.

18-105 f/3.5: The standard 'kit lens' that accompanies some of the entry level models by Nikon, this is perhaps the most versatile of all the cameras due to its low price and range of abilities such as zoom and wide angles.

Accessories

A set of accessories that support the imaging capabilities of the camera are an absolute must for every photographer. The number and types of accessories that you take along with you depends on the quality of the photos that you intent to capture. For example, if you tend to take regular, enthusiast level pictures than a camera bag, flash and extra memory would be enough. However, if you are looking to base your trip on the photography, you will need some extra supporting accessories in your kit.

Following are some of the accessories that any serious photographer must have with them if they are to take the best possible photos at Disney.

Tripod/Monopod: Every photographer, no matter how proficient, needs a decent stability support system to use for shots that require zero camera movement. A tripod can be used for total stability, for photos that require a very stable base, such as low light shots or those with rapidly moving objects. The monopod will help you get more creative angles, while allowing you to rotate and tilt the camera from the single support leg, making it more flexible.

Camera Bag: A decent sized bag can hold all of your equipment within reach, while you take photos. The best bags have multiple compartments for all sorts of items such as laptops and even water bottles and such. If you are looking for an all-in-one carry solution, go for a bag that has an attachment for the tripod as well.

Extra Memory: Having to delete some photos to make room for more is a big inconvenience. Fortunately, there are bigger and more spacious flash memory devices and even external drives available that support almost all DSLR models and makes. It is a good idea to take at least a 500GB memory drive with you. This can serve as a folder for the rest of your photos too, due to the ample capacity.

Sturdy Strap: Any photographer needs something that will let them have the camera within reach while not having to hold in hand all the time. A strap can make your life easier in this way, and the sturdier the strap, the more secure it will be. A strap can also prevent accidents, in case you lose your grip on your camera and drop it accidentally.

External Flash: A good flash will let you fill in light while not making the subject look to harshly lit. The flash that comes built-in to the camera is usually of terrible light quality. This is a good reason for you to invest in an external flash attachment. You can even attach diffusers to the flash, to spread the light evenly and soften it a bit, so as to appear soft and natural. Key point to remember, never use flash on dark rides. This ruins the effect along with the experience for other patrons.

Now that you have your ideal kit with you, you are prepared to take pictures like a pro. More than anything though, you have to realize that photography is more about intuition than equipment. Even if you have the most basic kit, you can still take some truly amazing photos, if you know how to approach the scene. And the following tips will help you learn just that.

Capturing Special Events

The world of Disney is known all over the world for hosting a number of live events and parades that are a very active attraction for visitors. As such, you will need to learn the nuances of each event and the sort of photographic conditions that you can expect while there.

To aid you in this, following are some guides for the most famous of live events and spectacles.

Fireworks Shows

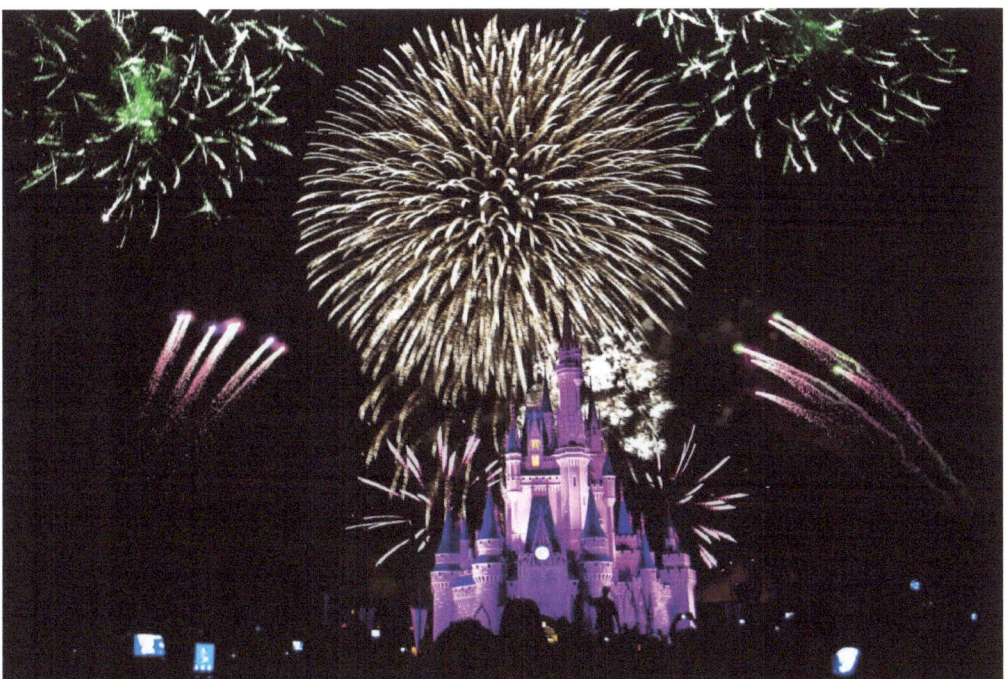

The fireworks shows at Disney take place daily not just a few times a year on special holidays and related national and international events. They do have special shows the most recent of such shows will be on the Halloween holidays, which are sure to draw out quite the crowd as always.

Fireworks shows and the fireworks themselves are unique in the sense that although they happen at night, in obviously low surrounding light conditions, the give off a considerable amount of light. Logic dictates that you use a lens with a very wide aperture setting for such conditions. However, for fireworks, you will need a zoom lens set to the infinity (∞) aperture setting.

Also important is the setting up of the camera and the composition. You will need to have access to a reasonably high vantage point to set the camera on the tripod. If the ground is uneven such as on a hill, you will need to adjust the tripod accordingly. Make sure that your tripod is set up and fixed tightly on all the extendable areas, so as to avoid shakes and sudden falls in height.

Additionally, it is a good idea to invest in a wireless remote, as they eliminate the possibility of shakes by hand.

How to set the camera up, settings wise, depends entirely on you and your preferences. If you want long, trailing lights and a light-graffiti effect, put the camera on the **Bulb** setting, with a 10-15 second shutter delay. If you want to catch the sparks and the bursting lights as they happen, set the shutter speed to 1-3 seconds. The later requires you to have a very quick response time as you will only have a split second to click the photo as soon as the fireworks burst. Use the lowest ISO setting your camera has and set the aperture around f/11-f/16 as a starting point.

For the focus, either set the distance on an object or a structure that is around the same distance as where the fireworks will start, or focus on the fireworks as soon as the start. Remember to always use a manual focus when shooting fireworks, to avoid autofocus disruption.

Finally, to optimize your shooting experience for fireworks, practice on a few of the initial volleys first, to get a feel for the reaction time that you need to possess and the ideal composition for the shots.

Following are some of the best spots at Disney's Magic Kingdom, for shooting fireworks displays.

- In font of Cinderella's Castle, standing right next to, or a few steps behind the Partners Statue. This will allow you to take advantage of the perspective distortion, capturing the display from the optimal angle.
- The FastPass viewing areas, which offer some decent setup space as well as a broader view of the fireworks display for some amazing landscape shots.
- The Hump, which is perhaps the best vantage spot, despite being somewhat crowded. The 'hump' on the main street makes this spot higher than the others, while still being a good distance from the Castle.

Meet and Greets

The Disney characters themselves are like walking photo opportunities, for both young kids and photography enthusiasts alike. For the little ones, it is a chance to meet all their favorite characters, for the photographer, it is an impromptu photoshoot with a willing model, and for the whole family, it is an all-round wonderful experience.

The best way to shoot a meet and greet with a character is to be prepared to frame and shoot instantly. Especially when there are children involved, you have to capture certain moments such as when they see the character up close for the first time, or when they hug them. The costumed people are very friendly, welcoming and affectionate, especially towards children, which will allow you to capture some truly heartfelt and warm moments.

Such photos warrant the need for the 50mm f/1.4 and a quick shutter. The f/1.4 will let you get an attractive, shallow depth of field with the character and the person in sharp focus, with minimal background and foreground visual interference. Additionally, this will allow you to shoot even when there are people in the background or the immediate foreground, as long as the characters are centered in the frame.

Finally, when they are ready to have their picture taken, wait for both the character and the person who is meeting them to get ready and pose. The people who play the characters are generally quite willing to let the photographer take some time to set up the perfect photo, which is a good reason not to rush this too much out of courtesy. You can also shoot action scenessuch as children pretending to have a sword fight or casting a spell, along with the characters.

You can use the f/1.4 once again for this photo, or opt for the 28-75 f/2.8 at the high end, to substitute for the comparatively smaller aperture with the zoom.

Parades and Parties

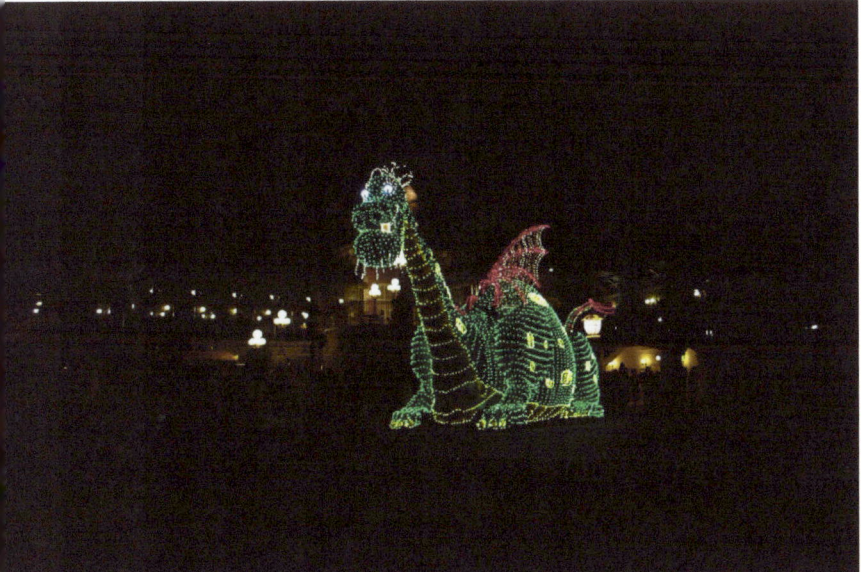

The parades at Disney are highly energetic and bright affairs, which regularly draw crowds in the hundreds. To make the most of time at such an event, photography wise, you have to work at it to make sure you have the ideal conditions.

First and foremost is getting in the best spot possible. When we talk about a Disney parade, the front row is the only spot worth considering. These spots are level with the procession itself and present some very good composition opportunities.

Try to avoid a spot that is higher than the level of the parade. You will end up with some quite unattractive photos with unappealing shadows and more of the background than what looks good.

The parades usually run along a fair bit of distance so you might want to scout your locations early on. Pick a god spot where you know there will be a less busy background and prepare your camera for daylight shooting. The aperture settings depend on how deep or shallow a focus field you want. Naturally this will affect the compositions themselves, as explained below.

If you are using a portrait lens such as an f/1.4 capable piece, try to shoot the members of the parade at the very front, as soon as they form a straight line in your field of vision. This means that although they will be in different positions on their end, they will align in a sideways line at some point, allowing you to apply sharp focus on them.

If you are using a slightly wider angle lens, make sure to fill the frame with the parade members with some empty space at the very right of the frame. Additionally, when using wide angles, it is always best to stand on the left side of the lane, if facing the parade. This allows you to take better looking sweeping shot as the left aligned angle is universally recognized as superior. Also, do not go over f/3.5 on the aperture with wide angle shots as these will distort the focus on the edge of the frame, due to those subjects being behind the centrally focused ones.

For shooting floats, especially those with characters on top, crouch down with the camera and shoot upwards. Try to get the main attraction of the float, such as the pumpkin shaped carriage enclosure in case of a Cinderella float, in the frame. This will allow you to add a bit of grandeur to the images.

If you are still in doubt, stick with the aperture priority setting till you get a feel for how the camera captures in which specific condition.

Capturing Specific Locations

Disney has a multitude of spectacular locations that are as magical as they are beautiful to look at and take pictures of. The best part about these locations is that you do not have to be a professional to take good photos there. All you need is a camera and some creative intuition to make your photos look beautiful. However, if you know how to take the picture and where to take the picture from, you can turn the clicking into an experience to remember.

Following are some tips on the ideal photography spots on each of and around the most famous locations, and some techniques to turn the magic up a notch!

Cinderella's Castle

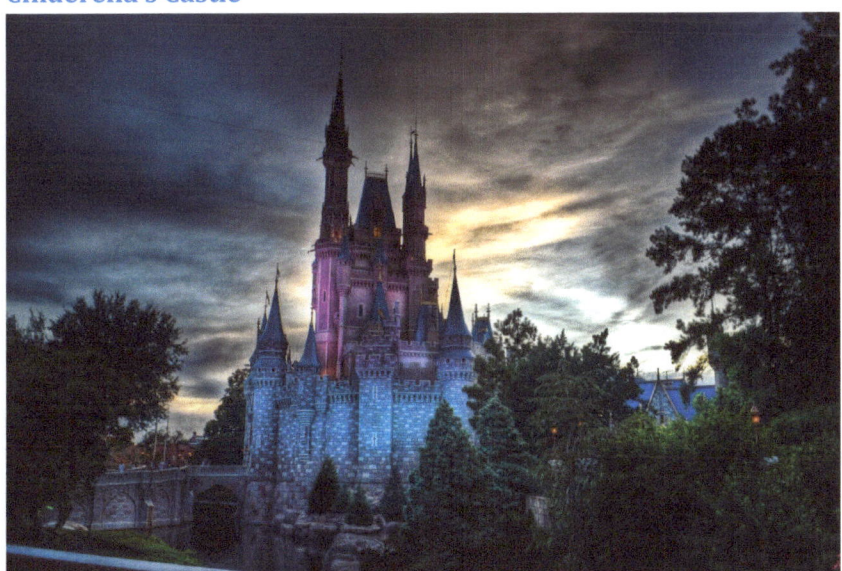

The Castle has been described according to various sources as the most shot place in the world. And for good reason, seeing as every single detail of the venue looks photo-ready, be it any lighting condition. There are some locations around the place that can make even the already brilliant photos look even better. Following are some of those spots.

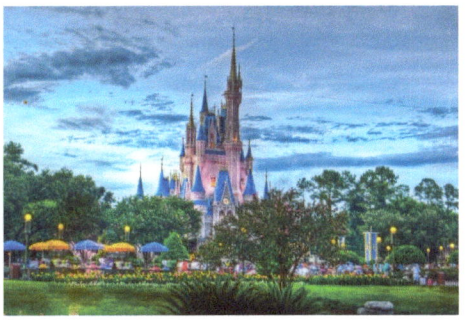
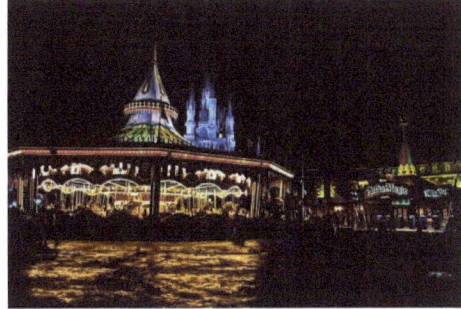

- The walkway that is directly between Fantasyland and Liberty Square is one of the least popular spots for photography, mainly because it is not known as much. There is some foliage and trees blocking the view but there is a break in the tree line here and there, which will let you capture some truly beautiful photos, especially during sunset. You will have some lens flare to deal with at this time so a UV filter is a good investment.
- Liberty Square Bridge presents somewhat similar lighting to the aforementionedwalkway, with the only difference being an even better view. As far as the park as a setup spot is concerned, you will not have a better view than from the Bridge. The surrounding moat will make a nice

addition to your frame, making the 18-105mm lens at the low range, the lens of choice for this shot.

- The Transportation and Ticket Center is another perfect spot for a wide angle shot with the zoom lens. The shot is perfect for the fireworks displays or just to see the Castle illuminated against the sky. The Center is a long way from the castle so you will need the 18-200mm or longer ranged lens for this.

Sleeping Beauty's Castle

This particular castle is not as grand or imposing as Cinderella's, but it has its own up's, especially if you like a bit of greenery around your subjects. However, if you know the spots to set up on, you can take equally breathtaking images of Sleeping Beauty's Castle as well.

Following are some of those spots.

- The Compass Rose is one of the more popular spots for photographers. However, the majority of people miss a wonderful feature to include in their photos, the Compass Rose itself. The trick is to aim the center spot in your viewfinder on to the tip of the middle compass needle, which inadvertently 'points' to the castle.
- Main Street end is another good spot, albeit with a swarm of visitors at most times. The Train Station's top serves as a good vantage point. It is not advisable to take a wide angle shot here though. Instead, go for a tighter frame on the Castle.
- You will find the inside of the castle, shot with the 18-105mm on the lowest range, to be one of the most beautiful photos on your entire visit. The best angle is the one that looks back towards Main Street.

Magic Kingdom Entrance

The Magic Kingdom entrance, although less popular a photography spot than Cinderella's Castle, is still an iconic venue. It is the symbol of Disney and the Mickey Mouse shaped flower garden; both represent the two things Disney is synonymous with.

You will notice that this guide is aimed mostly at locations inside the Magic Kingdom, with the exception of Sleeping Beauty's Castle. This is because of the overall grandeur of Walt Disney World and the Magic Kingdom itself.

For the perfect composition of the entrance, stand directly in front of it, setting up a low-angle shot. This is best done at night, when it is brightly illuminated. Use the 28-75mm f/2.8 at the low end for this shot.

To make the session truly iconic though, you will need to retreat back a bit, to get the entrance in full view. Once again, take a low-angle photo, framing the complete entrance while taking care not to get too many of the visitors' heads in your shot.

The fireworks display at the entrance the single iconic of all Disney imagery, as far as the movies are concerned, being the cinematic that plays at the start of every Disney movie.This makes the entrance shot with the fireworks, perhaps the most important photo you will take throughout your trip.

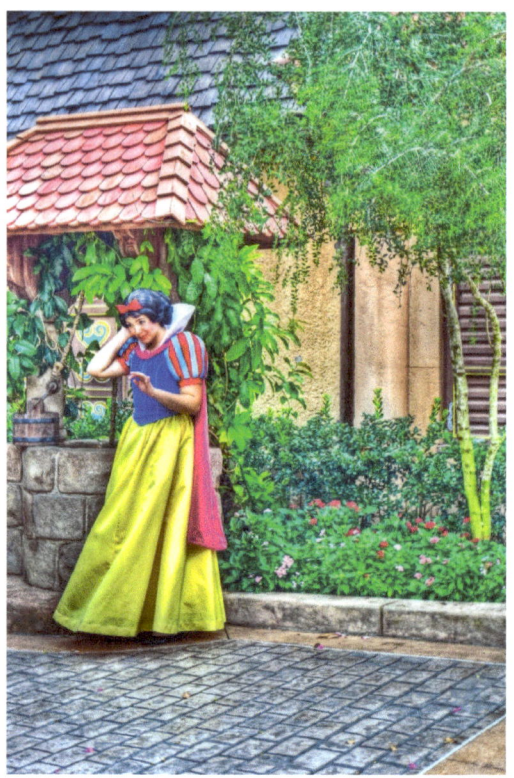

Character Portrait Composition

The beloved characters of the world of Disney are one of the main attractions at all the parks worldwide. More than anything, they are a chance to see the characters come to life in the most real way possible.

The camera settings and the compositions depend on where the photo is being taken, as well as the character itself. The latter requires a bit of thought behind it, as you will want to capture the character's story, based on the location.

If you are visiting for the first time, it will be beneficial to keep the camera at the aperture priority setting, to learn more about the ideal shutter speeds to use at a specific aperture value.

For the most part, it is important to compose the picture and shoot at the right moment. If you are shooting the characters with kids or other family members alongside them, either click at heartfelt moments when the characters hug or shake hands with the children, or afterwards when they are ready for the picture. Remember that behind the costumes are some extremely professional people who know how to pose for a photo. Do not rush the photo,instead, take your time to compose and be sure to thank the character after. Remember when taking photographs of children you should get down to their level.

Composing Shots According to A Character's Nature

The nature of the character in question is another very important factor that you have to take into consideration. The majority of the characters are quite happy to have their picture taken with anyone. In fact, they even react very true to the nature of their animated counterparts. This demands that you capture the essence of the character in every picture, instead of simply asking them to stand still and smile.

For this, you will have to gauge the surrounding of the character while having some knowledge of what the actual cartoon characters were like. While this may seem a bit excessive, to go to all this trouble for a photo, it simply wouldn't be doing justice to the character and indeed the world of Disney itself.

As mentioned earlier, you will need to capture a bit of the story behind the character.

For example, if you are photographing Gaston, you will want to do so with the famous Tavern in the background (also note this is a great place to photograph the fireworks show). This gives both a nice, rustic background to your picture, while telling a story about the character as well. Compose a picture with the character alongside a family member in a way that you get the front of the Tavern clearly in the picture. Use enough depth (aperture setting at f/16, shutter speed at 100, ideally) to sharply define the character as well as the Tavern itself.

Similarly, if you are photographing Ariel in the Grotto, you will need to consider the vibrant colors in the indoor setting, and feature some of the surrounding ambience in the photo. Once again, you will have to capture enough depth to define the character and some of the background. However, due to this being an indoor location, use the lower aperture setting such as the f/3.5.

Portrait and Full-Body Techniques

Portraits are best done with the 50mm f/1.4 lens, because of the shallow depth of field that the lens is capable of capturing. While the other lenses can also be used to shoot close-ups and portraits, the f/1.4 excels at this. The zoom range is perfect for portraits and the large aperture makes photos in low light a breeze.

Once again, the nature of the character can be used to your advantage here, for creative framing. For example, if the character is a prince, zoom in till only their torso is in the frame, move the frame to one side so that they have some space to gaze away into. This brings a more 'heroic' feel to the photo, while polishing your portraiture skills as well.

In the case of a princess, take a full body shot that shows their gowns sashaying about, giving the photos a more whimsical feel to them, true to the nature of the princesses. While shooting a moving shot such as you would with a princess, have the camera at the aperture priority setting for quicker shooting. Also, observe the settings that your camera does for that particular scene, and try to replicate them, slightly changing a few if you wish.

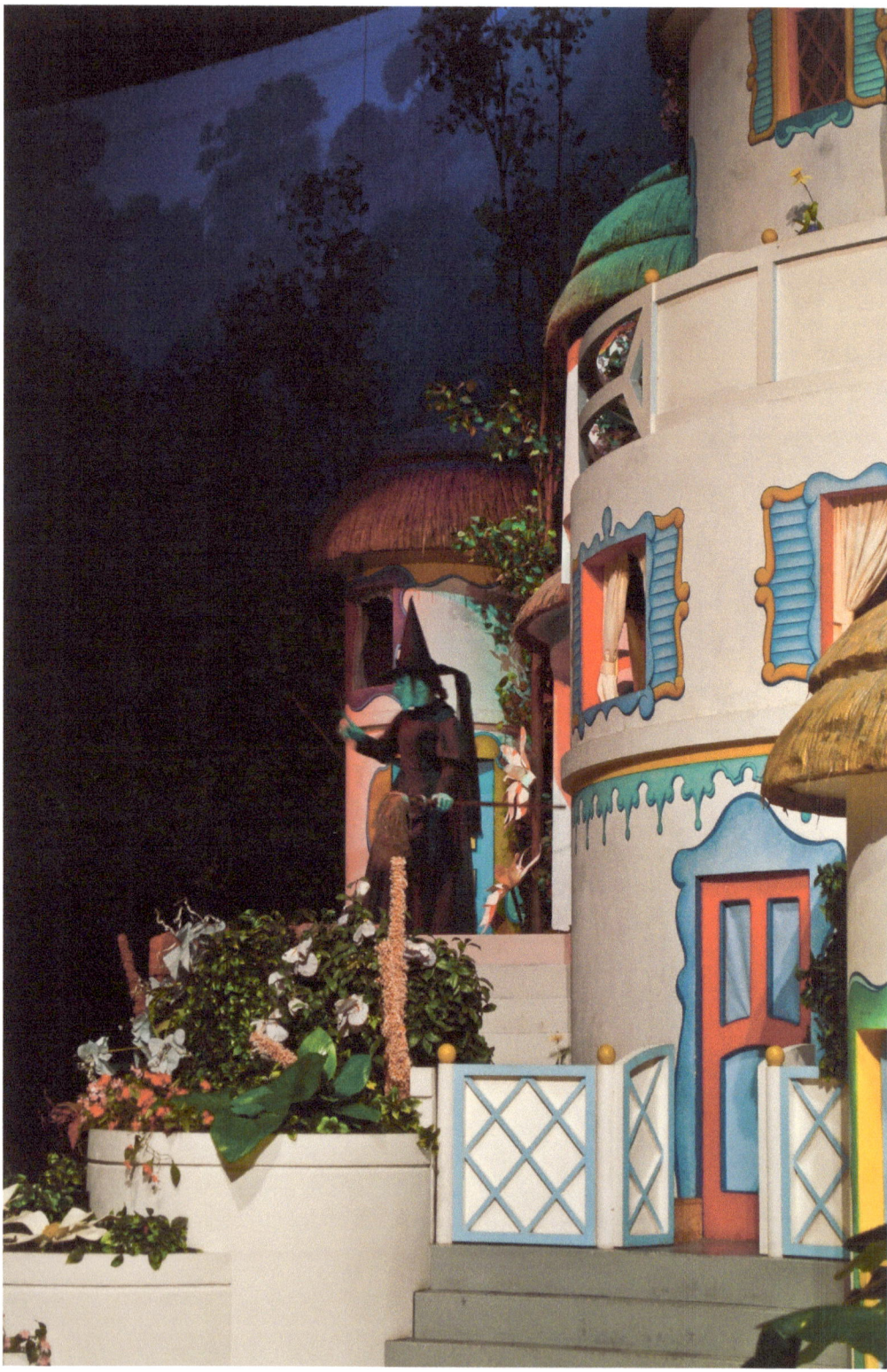

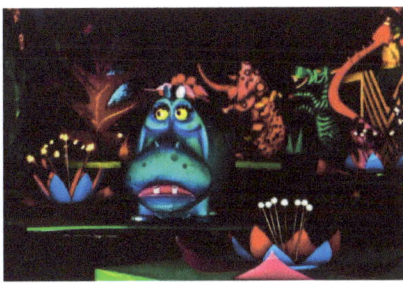

Low Light Photography at Disney

Low light photography in general is quite the art form, not to mention one of the toughest techniques to master, enough to run on manual mode.

Surprisingly enough, the manual mode is ideal for low light images, seeing as it gives you much more control over the kind of photos that your camera puts out. The plethora of settings in manual mode can get a bit confusing though, which is why you should start out with aperture priority and gradually work your way to manual. To learn more check out the rest of the series starting with "Photography 101" or visit www.RyanCranePhotography.com and improveyourphotographyonline.com.

In any case, if you are visiting Disney for the first time with the intention of bringing back a portfolio of photos, following are some beneficial tips for you.

Capturing Nighttime Landscapes

Tripods; this is the first and most important necessity for nighttime landscapes. Be it a tripod, stability bag, or any other implement that ensures photo stability, you are going to need it for landscapes at night.

The best part about night landscapes is that they can be taken with very little effort, once you get accustomed to the settings of your camera. You will also need a good zoom lens such as the 18-200mm to make the most of the landscape. The 18mm low end will let you get some very wide angles and the 200mm high end will let you zoom in on a subject that is very far away, while retaining some frame integrity.

One technique that is popular among photographers is the long shutter or long exposure. When you open your shutter for a couple of seconds at a time, you essentially allow more light to fall on the sensor. This brings out a brighter image with some very vivid colors. This technique is very effective if you dislike having a high ISO, which results in grainy images.

Optimal Settings for Low Light Photography

The extent of the setting that need to change for low light imagery depends on the conditions and some other variables, such as the amount of support equipment you have and how capable you camera and lenses are.

The camera itself is often disregarded in this aspect. It is a popular notion that the lens and the photographer are more responsible for the outcome of the photo. However, the more high-end your camera is, the better the sensor you will have in your arsenal. And the better your sensor, the less you have to decide on ISO and long exposures to capture more light. Even with high-end equipment you will want to use the lowest ISO setting and a wide aperture as well. This will enable you to use the camera's own ability capture light, while eliminating any excessive noise.

If the scene is well lit, you can use the surrounding light to your advantage. How bright the lights are and how neutral they are will decide how much aperture you should use. For such conditions, use only the aperture to compensate for the low lights. This, while giving you a shallow depth of field, will make sure that you do not have to turn the ISO up or the shutter speed down. However, even if you have aperture at the highest setting, sometimes it is not enough. In those cases, it becomes necessary to increase the shutter speed, which then makes the imagery more susceptible to shakes.

To combat this, you will need a sturdy tripod and lower the shutter speed to the appropriate level. For example, if the only lighting available to you is from the stars, set the shutter speed to as low as ½, or even lower, if you want a brighter picture. Remember that even if you have a low shutter speed, sometimes grainy images are unavoidable, which is why you need to keep the ISO to the lowest possible level, to avoid further noise.

To capture the starburst pattern in every singular light spot, increase the aperture value to 16 or higher. The tiny gaps between the overlapping aperture plates within the lens enclose light between them, making a starburst shape on every individual spot of light.

How to Correctly Use Flash

Using a flash outside a studio is widely considered a sin by photography puritans. This is mainly because it is a 'cheap' and unattractive way to compensate and fill light. There are very few implements that you can use to reduce the visually negative effects of the harsh, white light emitted by the majority of flashes.

Diffusers are one such implement. There are a variety of diffusers that you can use and they come in all shapes and sizes. The sort of diffuser you take along with you depends on the strength of your flash, but it is a good idea not to take anything too bulky like an oversized dome or reflector.

A diffuser cap that is not too dull and pasty will be perfect for flash photography in places where you need just enough light to naturally illuminate the scene without it looking overly artificial. If you are looking for more surface area for even more diffusion, opt for a collapsible diffuser with at least three sections that open out.

It is important to know that using a flash takes away a significant amount of the photo's integrity as a work of art. Try to avoid bringing out the flash as much as possible, using it only when it is otherwise not possible to get an aptly lit image.

Additionally, using a flash on rides that are dark and intentionally low-lit is an absolute travesty. It is an inconvenience to almost everyone in your immediate vicinity, not to mention incredibly rude. More than just rides, it is not suitable to use flash in areas that are intentionally dark or that feature some sort of dramatic lighting. To learn more regarding how and how not to use flash, read the blog regarding flash photography in Disney, on http://www.ryancranephotography.com/and visit http://improveyourphotographyonline.com/ for tutorials and further techniques.

Action Shots

When at Disney, chances are that you will get up to a lot of excitement, even if you are visiting purely as a photographer. The magical aura of the place is likely to sweep you up and tempt you to be part of the action whenever you can.

In such an event, it is a very smart move to have the equipment ready and at hand for some fantastic action shots of rapidly moving objects and characters, as well as rides.

Following are some tips on how you can capture the action at its finest.

How to Capture Moving and Action Shots

The f/1.4 lens is once again the tool of choice here. These lenses are referred to as 'fast lenses', due to their ability of producing a similar level of exposure while enabling you to shoot at much higher shutter speeds.

Certain brands of lenses also have bigger overall diameters. Brands like Tamron have always excelled in this area. Their lenses have a faster autofocus as well, adding to the already superior shooting speed that comes with the f/1.4.

During daylight conditions, if it is a character that is moving, you will need to compose the shot very quickly. This means that you will have to read their movements and judge where in the frame they should be, within seconds. This manner of thinking on your feet will come instinctively to you, once you become proficient.

Because action shots require a bigger aperture to allow for the necessary shutter speeds, the bare minimum aperture that you should go for is the 3.5. Anything below that will darken the photo excessively.

If you are taking action shots at night, you will need a very steady hand and some on-the-spot intuition. Having a good light source nearby is beneficial, as it will allow you to capture people with more natural (pertaining to the surroundings) skin tones.

Taking Photos on Rides

And now we come to the toughest part of the photography experience; capturing magical shots while on a dark ride. There are quite a few of those at Disney, and if you do not possess the right tools and knowledge, you might make a colossal mess out of both your own experience, as well as that of many other people.

As we talked about earlier, using flash on dark rides is looked down upon as one of the biggest faux pas at Disney. If your need for illumination is that great, either increase the white balance in your camera, or don't shoot at all. The sudden burst of light is very unseemly, especially when the surroundings are intended to be this dark. This takes away the ambient charm and excitement of the location.

As far as settings are concerned, this is one area where it is better to shoot in raw, with white balance set to auto. This will make your images much easier to edit, as well as more defined.

Another very important factor for consideration is the metering. If you are using a Nikon DSLR, set the metering mode to **Spot**. In case of a Canon, set it to **Partial Metering**. This lets you put maximum metering focus on the spot at the center of your frames.

The rides at Disney are mostly dramatically lit with some lights being brighter and with dimmer lights surrounding them. Take your photos with the spot in your viewfinder on these bright lights. Doing so will result in a more appealing photo, while the metering focus on the center will eliminate the chances of the subjects being overexposed, as happens in the default metering.

Lowering the exposure compensation is another technique that will prevent overexposed images. You can always fix the shadows in the editing phase. A value of -0.7 to -1.7 is ideal.

Last but not least, we have the focus, which will be working near constantly throughout the ride while you are snapping. The AF-C setting in Nikon DSLRs and Servo setting in Canon, will help you in this manner considerably, since it will track focal points by itself, making for some dynamic moving shots.

If you are feeling adventurous, try out manual focus as well. It is extremely difficult, if not completely impossible, to take a perfectly focused moving shot in manual mode. It is however a wonderful chance to polish your skills as a photographer.

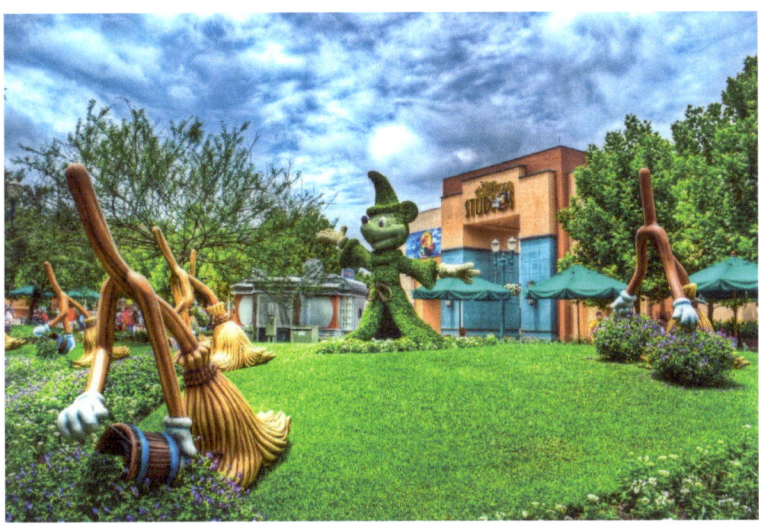

HDR Photography at Disney

HDR is the subject of quite some controversy within the photography community worldwide. While some swear by the results that it produces, some are in favor of the more puritan style of shooting an image once, depending solely on one's skills and the ability of the equipment.

HDR stands for High Dynamic Range. This basically refers to the saturation and the tonal definition of the photo. When you take a photo of an object or a scene, your camera captures the image according to the various settings that have been implemented. If the shutter speed is slow, the photo will be bright and vice versa. However, if you take several photos of the same object or scene, at different shutter speeds, and combine them into one photo; it has the effect of adding definition to the shadows as well as the highlights of the photo.

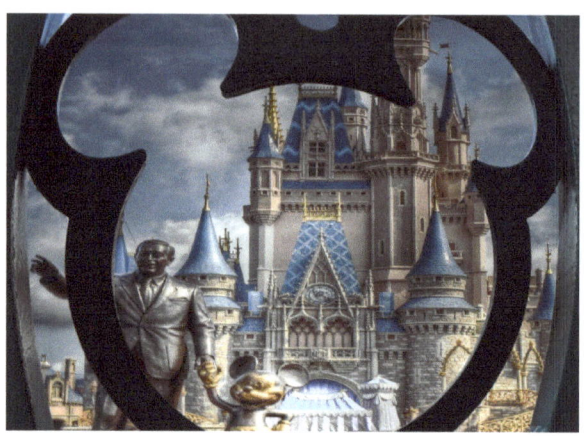

This is done by software in post-production, by combining the features of a dark, medium and bright image, to create a very high dynamic range.

Disney has no shortage of areas that could benefit from this style of imagery. The bright lights and incredibly varying areas, shadows and highlights wise, make this almost a necessity, if you like your photos vibrant and clearly defined, and don't mind them looking fake and heavily retouched.

The software that is ideal for this purpose include Adobe Photoshop, Photomatix, Lightroom and many others. If you are shooting in raw, open the image in Adobe Camera Raw. This will make the job a lot easier as minimal editing will be required later on when you open in Photoshop, or your preferred software.

To learn more about HDR techniques and what it entails, check out my book '**Gearing up for HDR Photography**', read the blog on HDR photography, on www.ryancranephotography.com, and visit www.improveyourphotographyonline.com for tutorials.

Conclusion

A good photographer can bring out the best in any venue or location, through their art. When visiting a land of magic and memories such as Disney however, the need to do so is tenfold. This is why you should brush up your photography skills before each visit. This will not only improve your overall skill, but make your experience at Disney a memorable one.

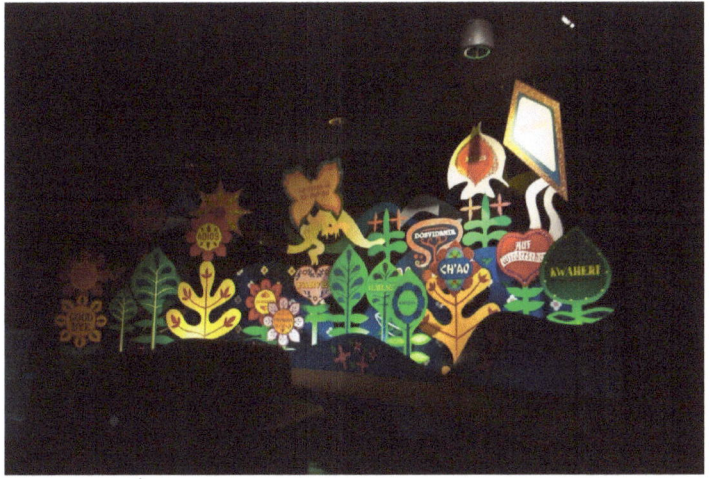

About the Author

Ryan Crane learned about photography by performing extensive research and then applying the learned principles in the field over a number of years. He is now a well renowned photographer and wants to help others become better at photography as well. He believes that you can become a better photographer, if you can work on your skills and follow the best advices that are on offer in the digital world.

One of the best sources in this regards is the http://improveyourphotographyonline.com/ website which allows you to learn through tutorials and different sessions.

Ryan tries to help inspiring photographers by providing them with a number of image resources such as backgrounds and tutorials. His work is available at http://www.ryancranephotography.com/ and can be viewed by any budding photographer.

www.ingramcontent.com/pod-product-compliance
Lightning Source LLC
Chambersburg PA
CBHW040915180526
45159CB00010BA/3076